KEEPING MY NAME

PREVIOUS WINNERS OF THE WALT MCDONALD
FIRST-BOOK COMPETITION IN POETRY

Strange Pietà GREGORY FRASER

Skin APRIL LINDNER

Setting the World in Order RICK CAMPBELL

Heartwood MIRIAM VERMILYA

Into a Thousand Mouths JANICE WHITTINGTON

A Desk in the Elephant House CATHRYN ESSINGER

Stalking Joy MARGARET BENBOW

An Animal of the Sixth Day LAURA FARGAS

Anna and the Steel Mill DEBORAH BURNHAM

The Andrew Poems SHELLY WAGNER

Between Towns LAURIE KUTCHINS

The Love That Ended Yesterday in Texas CATHY SMITH BOWERS

KEEPING MY NAME

Catherine Tufariello

Introduction by Robert Fink

TEXAS TECH UNIVERSITY PRESS

This book is typeset in Minion. The paper used in this book meets the minimum
requirements of ANSI/NISO Z39.48-1992 (R1997). ∞

Library of Congress Cataloging-in-Publication Data
Tufariello, Catherine.
Keeping my name / Catherine Tufariello ; introduction by Robert Fink.
    p.   cm.
ISBN 0-89672-529-4 (cloth : alk. paper)
1. Women—Poetry. 2. Women in the Bible—Poetry. 3. Love poetry,
Italian—Translations into English. I. Title.
PS3620.U36K44 2004
811'.6—dc22
2003023043

Printed in the United States of America

03 04 05 06 07 08 09 10 11 / 9 8 7 6 5 4 3 2 1

Texas Tech University Press
Box 41037
Lubbock, Texas 79409-1037 USA
800.832.4042
ttup@ttu.edu
www.ttup.ttu.edu

For my parents and sisters,
and for Jeremy

Acknowledgments

The author gratefully acknowledges the following publications in which some of these poems and translations first appeared:

The Dark Horse (Scotland): "Elegy for Alice," "Moving Day," "Snow Angel," and "Two Trees"

The Formalist: "Chemist's Daughter," "First Contact," "Ghost Children," and "The Mirror"

The Hudson Review: "Free Time," "The Walrus at Coney Island," and the translations of Cavalcanti's "Beltà di donna e di saccente core" and Petrarch's "Or ài fatto l'estremo di tua possa"

Italian Americana: "Lorenzo Lotto's *Annunciation*"

Poetry: "The Feast of Tabernacles," "February 18, 1943," "Fruitless," "In Glass," and "The Waiting Room"

Sparrow: "Pentimento," "Plot Summary," and the translation of Petrarch's "Se la mia vita da l'aspro tormento"

Tar River Poetry: "Useful Advice"

Yale Italian Poetry: Translations of Guinizelli's "Al cor gentil ripara sempre Amore" and Petrarch's "S'amor non è, che dunque è quel ch' io sento?" and "I dì miei più leggier che nesun cervo"

"After All" first appeared in *The New Penguin Book of Love Poetry*, edited by Jon Stallworthy (Penguin U.K., 2003). "No Angel," I-VI, "Rebekah I," "Rebekah II," and the translation of Petrarch's "Ite, rime dolenti, al duro sasso" first appeared in *Annunciations* (Aralia Press, 2001). "Dana Dancing," "Keeping My

Name," and "Seasons of the Moon" first appeared in *Free Time* (Robert L. Barth, 2001).

Some of the botanical details in "Florida's Flowers" were drawn from Winston Williams's book *Florida's Fabulous Flowers: Their Stories* (World Publications, 1999).

Contents

Introduction

CATHERINE TUFARIELLO's lyrical collection of metrical, formal poems, *Keeping My Name,* may have arrived for you, as it did for me, just in time. In a world increasingly inclined toward terror and self-destruction, *Keeping My Name* celebrates, in musical, imagistic poems, lavish, resilient love ("After All"). And, as you know, love that survives, that turns out *true,* is complex with "delight and outrage" ("Free Time"), "giddy with boldness and vertigo" ("February 18, 1943"). It is a love defined by "playfulness and pluck" ("Epitaph for a Stray"), the joy of a young girl dancing by herself—"a little universe / That swells, contracts, and never tires of turning" ("Dana Dancing").

It arrives at the most unexpected moments and to the most unexpected people—those whose lives are a history of "small ordinary decencies" ("Twenty Weeks"), those who "could never hope to win / The hearts of strangers" ("A Proposal in the Cleveland Museum, Winter 2000"). This love is tumultuous, "terribly real," its recipients instinctively raising their hands "protectively. . . . eyes wide with apprehension and surmise" ("Lorenzo Lotto's *Annunciation*"). It comes as a "miracle redeeming all their years / Of numbing tedium" ("A Proposal in the Cleveland Museum, Winter 2000"). It is the salvation of "unremembered ones" ("Elegy for Alice"), those who have always understood "what Hope was doing in Pandora's jar" ("The Waiting Room"), who have "slowly learned love's alphabet" ("First Sight").

Theirs, ours, is a "story full of surprises after all" ("Plot Summary"), a tale of "curious intimacies" in a neighborhood of telephone party lines ("Crossed Wires") where, after grief and loss, after "the dumb resurgence and the death of hope," we discover that greater than faith, than hope, is love—"how lavish, how resilient" ("After All").

As with each of the previous books in The Walt McDonald First-Book Poetry Series, *Keeping My Name* is a carefully orchestrated, thematically linked collection. The five sections showcase Catherine Tufariello's repertoire of poetic forms and styles—from blank verse to rhymed couplets, to villanelles, to sonnet sequences, to women of the Bible persona poems, to translations of Italian love sonnets.

The poems progress section by section through stages of loss and love, celebrating the play, the dance, the joy (though often momentary) of *free time*—time out from our "long-confirmed routine" ("The Walrus at Coney Island"), from the end of "a run of luck" ("Epitaph for a Stray"), from the dark that "stalks you on its silent paws" ("Two Trees"), a sister who "wore her body down to bone" ("Snow Angel"), the husband who says he does not think he wants to be married to you "any more" ("The Mirror"), ghost children "whose faces are mirrors of all we've lost" ("Ghost Children"), the waiting room of "blank-faced commuters rumbling underground" ("The Waiting Room"), well-meaning friends who say, "You mind my asking, is it him or you?" ("Useful Advice"), the "whole ordeal . . . darkly funny" ("After All").

These are hard-wrought love poems acknowledging zero at the bone, having gone "beyond despair" ("After All") to discover, "as you deplored your lot," the "cunningly constructed door" always there but unseen; and now, "stricken with wonder," you find it is unlocked and "yields beneath your hand" ("The Dream of Extra Room") to open on a new, fruitful marriage, a beautiful midsummer daughter—"Marvelous as an unexpected joke, / A gift to be unwrapped" ("This Child"). The dreamed face of love surfaces "bruised and wet," no longer a ghost—"Substantial now as any stone" ("First Sight"), as the name by which we are known.

ROBERT FINK
Abilene, Texas, 2004

I

Free Time

Free Time

Their shrieks careening dizzily between
Delight and outrage, the students in the yard
Are playing hard,
Though they have little room and nothing green
In their asphalt pen. Nothing but fences, bricks,
And at regulation height, a pair of hoops
From which gray loops
Vestigially descend. With graceful flicks
And swoops they pass, block, feint and argue fouls,
And all the while the staccato, meaty thwack—
Now quick, now slack—
Thrums on, a backbeat to their cheers and howls.

Three stories up, on her habitual perch,
A black-and-white cat observes the scene,
Brushing the screen
With down-curved whiskers, rapt in scan and search
As though the swirl below were birds or fish.
In the cacophony, it seems she hears
The singing spheres,
Each ear a separately tuning radar dish.

I join her at the window, and together
We watch the game until the tardy bell,
Whose clanging knell
Recalls them, some still wrangling over whether
The last shot counted. In the sudden peace,
A handyman, belt slung with rules and hammers,
Appears and clambers
Onto the gym roof. While a scrawl of geese
Ripples on windy gray in ragged flight,
He gathers up the balls that got away
And spent the day
Aimlessly free—red, orange, purple, white—

And punts them, in bright arcs, back into play.

February 18, 1943

In memory of Hans and Sophie Scholl,
leaders of the White Rose student resistance movement,
executed February 22, 1943.

I imagine how easily you could have gotten away,
Standing in the Ludwigstraße in the sun
That improbably springlike February day,
The not-quite-empty suitcase slung
Between you—like two students on holiday,
Let out of class, on your way to catch a train.
Relieved and out of breath,
You stood for a moment blinking in the sun,
Tasting the early spring that caught all Munich unawares
After bleak weeks of cold.
How hopeful the light must have looked, how far from death.
Was it that you suddenly felt young?
—Another nose-thumbing at the omnipotent State!
Or was it the recklessness of the desperate?
Not furtively, but in the pale spun-gold
Of full daylight, like farmers casting grain,
You'd left your leaflets scattered on the floors
In the hallways, on windowsills, at the doors
Of the lecture rooms, and, ignoring their stony stares,
In the marble laps of Ludwig and Leopold.
Was it the change in weather
That made your glances catch, a glance that said
Almost gaily, *Why waste any?* so that instead
Of slipping away as planned, you raced together
Back to the empty hall,
And up the stairs, to let the last ones fall?

I imagine, then, how you leaned from the great height
Of the gallery railing into a well of light;
How, giddy with boldness and vertigo,
You popped the latch, and—hurriedly this time—scooped
The leftover handfuls out.

For a few seconds, the pages must have swooped
Like wind-torn blossoms, sideways in the air,
Filling the gallery with a storm of white,
While under the skylight with its square of blue
Your arms were still flung wide;
And while, rounding a corner down below,
For just a moment, the porter, Jakob Schmid,
Must have stopped to stare,
Not indignant yet, but merely shocked,
Blinded for an instant by the glare,
Before he recovered himself and did
His job as he'd been taught;
Before milling students spilled into the hall
From morning lectures, but not quite fast enough;
Before Schmid gave a shout,
And surging forward in the tumult, caught
The dark-haired young man's shoulder in a rough
Policeman's grip that would not be shaken off,
Though he didn't try, and the girl stayed by his side;
Before, in a sudden hush, the crowd withdrew,
And the doors all locked.

Elegy for Alice

I always assumed you were somewhere in the world,
And that someday we'd find each other again
And tell our adventures, like happy heroes
Reunited after years of wandering.

Hard to believe it's been a dozen years
Since we slogged together through the *Iliad*,
Longer than the whole of the Trojan War,
Or the wanderings of Odysseus afterward.

When your mother told me you were dead,
All I could think about was our favorite verb,
Μέλλω, our rueful shorthand for regret,
To be about to do, but leave undone.

"I meant," you'd say, "to study Greek last night,"
And I'd reply, "I too, O Agathon,
Intended to accomplish many things
Before the light of rosy-fingered dawn."

And now it's seven years that you've been gone.
While I was living my ordinary life,
And carelessly, fondly imagining you in yours,
(Losing, in one of my many moves, the funny,

Wonderful letters you wrote me from Mexico),
I never dreamed that you would not grow old,
That time had stopped for you as suddenly
As for the daughters of weeping Hekabe

In burning Troy—the unremembered ones
You summoned from the ashes in the fall
Of 1983, when you were asked
To translate the catalogue of Priam's sons.

Hard to believe that you will not return
And tell your adventures in the other world,
No matter how tenderly I brush the dead
Leaves from your sleeping face, and call your name.

Dana Dancing

While her older brother and sister run off to explore
This former mansion turned reception hall,
(Whose upstairs shadows beckon and appall),
Oblivious, serene, she takes the floor

And dances by herself in a forest green
Velvet dress with a snowy flounce of lace,
White tights, black patent leather shoes. Her place
A mere few months ago was still between

Her parents when the music played, but now,
Under the changing light, she slowly whirls
While her skirt fills like a sail. At two, her curls
Are nothing but a gosling fuzz, her brow

As large and solemn as the deep-set eyes
Fixed on her flaring dress. She has no winning
Ways to waste on us, intent on spinning
In a small secluded corner of the skies,

While her beaming cousin takes, for better or worse,
Her first steps with the groom. She'll soon be learning
The intricate *pas de deux* of love and yearning,
But for now she's still a little universe

That swells, contracts, and never tires of turning.

THE WALRUS AT CONEY ISLAND

He lumbers into view at 2:15
Precisely, by a long-confirmed routine,
And barking hoarsely, slowly hoists himself
Into position on the rocky shelf
Where lunch is served—a shambling, bald, obese
Old man in slippers, knowing no release
Will come from jostling kids who crane and shriek
While harried parents smile. He's made to speak
For smelt and herring, which he gobbles whole
With comic slurps. His upturned face—the droll
Mustache and beard, the mournful bovine eyes—
Seem out of keeping with his giant size,
The dead, trapped power of the massive tail
Scraped audibly on rusty stone. The pail
Soon emptied, and the task of eating done,
His strength gives way: he crumples in the sun,
His skin an old tarpaulin's mottled brown.

Then, when the handler gives the order—*Down!*—
And gestures to the pool, we catch our breath;
So perfectly he holds the pose of death,
We half-believe he'll never move again.
Once more the order's given. Only then
He stirs and lifts his head, heaving his wrecked
Resistant body wearily erect
And lunges as directed to the ledge,
Pausing to peer an instant from the edge.
All watchers gasp together as he dives,
The clumsy forefins clever now as knives,
The dark head bobbing in the dazzling spray
Of sun-shot water, like a child's at play.
So this is what he is, has always been:
A gleaming, sleekly muscled submarine,
Lithe as a dancer, roguish as a boy,
Corkscrewing downward with what looks like joy.

Epitaph for a Stray

Here lies Bottlebrush the cat,
Who had a friend in every house,
And could reduce a catnip mouse
To fuzz in sixty seconds flat.

Lots of things he didn't have—
A home, good looks, or many years,
A pedigree or prudent fears,
A collar or a proper grave.

But he had playfulness and pluck,
Street savvy, skill in all the arts
Of drawing and subduing hearts,
And for a while, a run of luck.

The day his luck ran out for good,
The friends he'd made (all strangers) cried,
And for a while, the night he died,
The street became a neighborhood.

CROSSED WIRES

Last night, I pick up the phone: a woman
With a heavy Brooklyn accent is discussing
With a friend how she managed to save a bundle
On a new sofa. Generous with advice
Like most New Yorkers, and unflappable—
She says when I remember my manners
And announce myself, *Well, whaddaya know.*
All day, no calls, and now a party line.
We exchange names—Mrs. Attanasio
Lives nearly a mile away, on Union St.,
But our wires are touching in some cable box
Says the brusque repairman. Just another
Of the curious intimacies of New York,
A city supposedly so anonymous
But where strangers learn each other's habits
Like the long married. Our pre-war building
Has sturdy walls, but still we can hear
Zachariah upstairs rolling his ball
And laughing, Diane in 3D rattling
Her pots and pans, Mrs. Cohen next door
Running water or clearing her throat
At night in the bathroom that abuts with ours.
Mrs. Murphy downstairs has lived here fifty years,
Was a WAVE in the War. She showed me a picture
Of her in her uniform—back straight, bright smile,
Dark curly hair. *Call me Marie,* she says.
She sits in the lobby all afternoon
With a wicker basket and skeins of yarn.
You didn't know now, did you dear,
All the lines in the neighborhood come in here.

II

Seasons of the Moon

CHEMIST'S DAUGHTER

Thumping the dinner table, Dad would say
it too was atoms—massed in galaxies
made mainly of empty space. At night, the bees'
drone of electrons woke me—a Milky Way
was whirling on the tip of my fingernail,
ten thousand planets dancing on its pale
half moon. Would bed, desk, dresser lose their grip
on the braided rug? Outside was empty space—
dark deserts stretched between the yellow face
of the moon and our backyard, where I would slip
through glittering snowcrust, playing astronaut.
The world looked solid. It was wild as thought.

MOVING DAY

Three, I watch her sweep
Each changed, familiar room,
And listen as the broom
Draws shadows out of sleep,

Its song the whisper of leaves
Whirling in papery swarms,
Of snow under sweeping arms.
Below, the furnace heaves

A sigh and so does she,
Still plying the rhythmic oar
That rows us over the floor,
Through the door, out to sea.

Two Trees

Every tree is two—the one
that spreads head upwards in the sun,

and another joined to it,
the first one's twin and opposite,

whose darker branches come and go,
swaying above, not under snow,

a map of veins on fainter blue,
a spider's web the wind slips through.

Sometimes it's a ship, a lean
ghost galleon on a sea of green,

sometimes a horse whose rippling mane
plunges over a windy plain,

sometimes a hive, a humming loom,
a ladder, a wave, a witch's broom.

You'll never scrape your knees to reach
smooth pear or caterpillar peach,

or rest high in its limber lap,
your fingers stained with sticky sap,

or hear it sobbing when it grieves,
or scuffle through its phantom leaves,

or swing, rough-palmed, from rougher boughs.
It will not hold a little house

for birds, or creak like Noah's ark.
You'll never see it in the dark

except by leaping firelight
or when the rising moon is bright,

and stealthily it creeps across
and stalks you on its silent paws.

Snow Angel

My sister wore her body down to bone
One winter while I lay and watched her sleep.
Through her thin shirt, I saw the wings she'd grown.

She was a child again, and then a crone
Bent to scour her stubborn flesh, to sweep
Her tender body clean as polished bone.

She clutched her fury like a sharping-stone,
Her will like some dark jewel she could keep
In secret, while she flexed the wings she'd grown.

My sister lay forgetting what she'd known—
Our private games, her rapturous wild leap
(With the joy of pounding blood and sturdy bone)

When we danced in summer storms, our nightgowns blown
Like sails. And laughed, collapsing in a heap,
As rain pulled down the heavy wings we'd grown.

She forgot the sweetness of a peach's stone
Sucked dry. And how to want, and how to weep.
Pale as the moon her body waned to bone.

I dreamed she woke me once. Her dark eyes shone
So strangely—open, though she was asleep.
On the glass behind her, ragged wings had grown.

She spoke then, in the new, dull undertone
I couldn't hear. The wind was herding sheep
And her body was his flute of hollow bone,

A body sharp-edged shadows had pared down
And bleached light pierced. The moon was poised to reap
The stars when she unfurled them, fully grown,

Chaste as moonlight, and as pale and lone.
While snow spun whitely, mothlike, soft and deep,
My sister wore her body down to bone.
Through her thin shirt, I saw the wings she'd grown.

Insomnia

Like a lighthouse stabbing through swaths of fog
The mind revolves, or a faithful dog
That turns and turns on the same worn round
Patch of the done day's rug, and will not lie down.

SEASONS OF THE MOON

The moon rose, a bright balloon slipped free
From a child's fist. A blue-tinged light, like milk,
Silvered their hair and turned the sheets to silk.
Still twined, they slept like children, knee to knee.

While plaintive crickets quavered in the yard,
The moon rose, a face half turned away
From the open window. Watching him, she lay
And wondered what it heard. She listened hard.

Wind tried the door all night, and dry leaves leapt
To peer inside, mice scrabbling at the screen.
A shell of moon appeared, washed pale and clean
Above the empty bed where neither slept.

They lay, two lovers carved in effigy
On a common tomb, awake in early dawn.
A few birds called across the snowy lawn.
Between the bare, clenched branches of a tree,

The moon slipped like a stone dropped in the sea.

THE MIRROR

The day after you say you do not think
You want to be married to me any more,
I meet my own dark gaze above the sink,
Surprised to find my image as before.
The mirror faithfully reflects my face,
My compact body, solid as a stone,
Familiar shapes your words did not erase,
A vacant house I do and do not own.
Yet I feel invisible, a fragile elf
Wandering rooms vivid with ghosts of you,
Unreal, spectral, even to myself,
Expecting strangers' eyes to run me through,
This stubborn flesh to meet dissolving air.
One day I'll wake, and no one will be there.

GHOST CHILDREN

Trying to offer comfort, friends remark
How lucky it is we never had a child.
I nod agreement, knowing in the dark
They'll wake me, wild, inconsolate. You smiled
Good-naturedly when we debated names
After the wedding, wondered whether your
Features or mine would make the stronger claims—
My hazel eyes? Your hair, a black so pure
It is tinged with blue? Back home in Hawaii, you said,
Hapa children are known for special beauty.
I hoped they'd have your cheekbones, and instead
Of my pale, your golden skin. Now I mourn the pretty
Darlings I carry but cannot have, the ghost
Children whose faces are mirrors of all we've lost.

The Worst of It

The worst of it is not the bitter shame
Of being left, but living a cliché.
"Good thing," my mother says, "You kept your name."
No thrill of wondering what the neighbors say,
But only the dull burden of our news
With power, perhaps, to sadden and surprise
But not to shock the hearers who must choose
Sides in our common struggle to revise
Our common story: we are the one of two
Couples in the marriage gamble who come to grief.
Too bad it didn't work; nothing to do
But wait for time's predictable relief.
I know these scenes, yet must enact them all
In our melodrama familiar and banal.

Pentimento

Our house still harbors memories of you
In haunting pentimento—like the faint
Unfocused images that flicker through
From a distant channel, or surface in the paint
Of a landscape grown translucent with the years.
A lake develops depths, from which a drowned
Nude body glimmers, or a dim face peers
Between two trees, half-hidden in the ground.
Fugitive shadow, fed on my regret,
Made strong by my refusal to forgive,
You inhabit the house in silvery negative.
How long before my body will forget
Your scent and touch, recorded in its pores?
How many times it held and harbored yours.

PLOT SUMMARY

This story is full of surprises after all,
That seemed in prospect so unpromising
I nearly closed the book. The lovers fall
In love on schedule, to be sure; and spring
Follows their winter of mutual despair
And reunites them, as we knew it would.
Put thus, the plot's familiar: nothing new there,
In the grand scheme. Look closer, now. Who could
Have guessed old Ivan had it in him to fall in love—
Really in love!— in the first place? Or that Anna,
So childlike and conventional, would prove
So brave? Canaan follows exile—but that manna
Would feed the wanderers? Oh, who would guess
Such bread could blossom in this wilderness?

KEEPING MY NAME

"T as in Tom . . . U . . . F as in Frank,"
I tell the voice at the bookstore or the bank,
Knowing the chances of its being right
On form or package are extremely slight
Unless the clerk repeats (and most don't bother)
This catechism I learned from my father—
T as in Tom, U, F as in Frank.
For this ritual I have myself to thank—
Twice I've had and forfeited the chance
To trade the burden and extravagance
Of five syllables for one or two.
I couldn't do it when I said "I do,"
Not even after three years in the South,
Where voweled names are mangled in the mouth.
What's in a name? Why, a family line,
Identity, tradition, but in mine
I had the gallop of the Latin dactyl;
Tufa, crumbly stuff, so richly tactile,
So unlike Grandpa's monumental granite;
And, from the intrepid who could scan it,
I had the liquid lilting of *iello*
(One teacher sang it sweetly as a cello);
And those plump vowels, juicy and alive—
At one per syllable, I had all five.
In school, through endless dreamy afternoons,
I brooded like a druid casting runes
Over the page to see how many words
My name would make, releasing them like birds
From the magician's cloak I always wore.
Every year they multiplied, to more
Than I'd thought possible, as *rat* and *tale,*
Tall and *tell* gave way to *trill* and *flail,*
If and *far* to *float, aloft* and *lift.*
One day a *rill* might bubble from a *rift,*

The next an *elf* warble a silver *lute*,
A leering *troll* swig *ale* or proffer *fruit*,
One taste of which might lead to *fault* and *fall.*
They scattered, and I catalogued them all:
Found *fore* and *after,* leaping *fire* and *air*
(With sandstone, all the elements were there),
Caught *Uriel,* Milton's angel of the sun,
Wearing cloudy *tulle,* and (nearly done),
Bright *Ariel,* Will Shakespeare's airy sprite,
Hidden in the middle, in plain sight—
Caught him in my net, then let him go,
Happy in his charms as Prospero.

III

"Go, grieving rhymes . . ."

TRANSLATIONS FROM THE ITALIAN

Beltà di donna e di saccente core

Guido Cavalcanti

A woman's loveliness, a wise man's heart,
Armed cavaliers in courtly gallantry,
The song of birds, sweet words when lovers part,
A fleet of gaily painted ships at sea,

The first clear light of dawn as darkness yields,
Snow floating slowly down in windless air,
The banks of streams, bright flower-studded fields,
Gold, silver, lapis, rich beyond compare;

My lady's beauty and her noble grace
And kindness so transcend these other charms
That they seem base in a beholder's eye.

So much more understanding lights her face
As earth is vaulted by the blazing sky,
And Goodness finds his refuge in her arms.

AL COR GENTIL RIPARA SEMPRE AMORE

Guido Guinizelli

To the gentle heart, Love comes to build his nest,
As circling birds fly to a forest's shade.
Before the gentle heart, Love was unguessed;
Till Love was born, the gentle heart unmade.
Even as the rising sun
Springs up with all the splendor of his light
At once, and neither one
Could shine alone, Love's nature must express
Itself in gentleness,
As heat's the core of hearthfires burning bright.

In love's clear fire the gentle heart transcends
Its flaws—in virtue like a precious stone,
To which no starry influence descends
Until the purifying sun has shone.
For when the sun draws forth
By force the final taint of what was base,
The star bestows its worth.
And thus the heart that Nature has designed
Confiding, chaste, and kind,
A woman, like the star, endows with grace.

Love makes its dwelling in the gentle heart
Like a candle's tip that flickers, clear and slight
Against the dark, and holds itself apart,
Too proud to shake except in self-delight.
When evil natures meet
Love's fire, they are as water that retains
Its chill, repelling heat.
But the gentle heart is Love's true complement;
They join in glad consent,
Like ore shot through, in mines, with diamond veins.

All day the sun beats down upon the earth:
Mud it remains, nor is the sun's heat less.
"Gentle am I," the proud man boasts, "by birth"—
Yet he is mud; the sun is gentleness.
Let no man dare to say
That the least gentility can be,
Even in a king's array,
Unless a gentle heart abides below.
Though waves wear starlight's glow,
Heaven holds the stars and their sublimity.

Beyond the spheres the world's Creator burns,
More splendid than the sun in human sight.
All heaven follows Him, and turning, learns
The radiance of uncreated light.
Even so light once obeyed
With instant joy its Maker's first decree.
And so my lady, rayed
With grace to all who see her, should impart
Her truth to one whose heart
Is hers, and who would serve her faithfully.

When my soul passes on the day of doom
Before God's throne and meets Him face to face,
He'll say in thunder, Lady, "You presume
To make vain love an idol in My place?
All honor men should give
To Me and heaven's Queen, against whose sword
Of love no sin can live."
Then I will plead, "O Lord, if I blasphemed,
Forgive me; but she seemed
An angel from Your realm, whom I adored."

FROM PETRARCH'S *Canzioniere*

S' AMOR NON È, CHE DUNQUE È QUEL CH' IO SENTO?

If not love, then what could this feeling be?
But if it's love, by God, what is this thing?
If good, why is its kiss a poison sting?
If evil, why is torment sweet to me?

If I burn willingly, then why lament?
And if against my will, why should I weep?
O living death, sweet fever, could you keep
Me captive still except with my consent?

And if I do consent, I must be brave.
Wind-buffeted, I sail without a helm
A ship each mounting wave would overwhelm,

So light in sense, so fraught with foolish yearning
I cannot even name the thing I crave,
In summer ice, and in deep winter burning.

SE LA MIA VITA DA L'ASPRO TORMENTO

O Lady, if my life can but withstand
These restless, bitter torments long enough
That I may see your eyes, the light I love,
Dimmed by Time's obliterating hand;

If I may live to see your golden hair
Made silver, see you lay aside your clothes
Of green and girlish garlands, while the rose
That eases grief, your cheek, turns pale with care;

Then Love, at least, at last will make me bold
To tell my sufferings—to let you see
How weary were these hours, days, and years;

And if Time proves my passion's enemy,
At least from sorrow he will not withhold
The solace of a few belated tears.

I DÌ MIEI PIÙ LEGGIER CHE NESUN CERVO

Swifter than deer, my days have taken flight,
Like shifting shadows winking in a wood,
And left behind them no enduring good
But thoughts of rare, sweet hours of cloudless light.

Desolate world, unsteady, hard as stone!
Whoever hopes in you is wholly blind.
In you my heart was lost, and lies consigned
To earth with her, now dust and nerveless bone.

And yet her soul survives; none can assail
Her place in highest heaven. I adore
Her beauty in its new form all the more,

And so I go, dim-eyed, hair silvered gray,
Rapt in the thought of where she lives today,
And in the brightness of her lovely veil.

OR ÀI FATTO L'ESTREMO DI TUA POSSA

Now you have done your utmost, cruel Death,
Now you have razed Love's kingdom, now your power
Has put out Beauty's light, destroyed her flower,
And in a narrow grave pent up her breath;

Now you have stripped our life of precious stones,
And gold, and honor's splendor; yet her fame,
Which never dies, escapes you all the same:
So you may keep, poor thief, the naked bones,

For Heaven holds the rest, and in her love
Exults as though it were a brighter sun;
And here the good will always sing her worth.

New angel, with the victory you've won,
Let pity for me fill your heart above,
As once your beauty vanquished mine on earth.

Ite, rime dolenti, al duro sasso

Go, grieving rhymes, and find the granite stone
That hides my dearest treasure underground
And call her there: her answer will resound,
Although dark earth has buried flesh and bone.

Tell her I can no longer live alone,
Braving these bitter tempests, nearly drowned,
But that, while scattered leaves fall all around,
I'll gather them and follow where she's gone,

Speaking only of her, who lives and dies,
(Or rather, who still lives and now is made
Immortal), that her fame will never fade.

And when my own death comes, may she arise
To meet me, taking mercy on my shade,
And draw me to her side in Paradise.

IV

Annunciations

Lorenzo Lotto's *Annunciation*

Other approaching Gabriels offer the lily
In a ceremonial hush to humble girls
Who bow their heads or touch their breasts. She whirls
Away as the angel runs in willy-nilly
And sinks to one knee, hair streaming—as if he hurries
To get there ahead of God, who stretches His arm
From a cloud in the doorway, while the striped cat scurries
For shelter, its tail an elongated S of alarm.

Hands raised protectively, she turns to look
Straight out at us—in shock, or mute appeal?
Forgotten behind her lies the open book.
In the tumult of the divine turned terribly real,
Only her face is strangely still, the eyes
Wide with apprehension and surmise.

A Proposal in the Cleveland Museum, Winter 2000

For Dick Davis, who told me this story

An easel's turned away
To face the wall between them—a benign
Virgin who watches while young shepherds pray,
And a swart bearded Bacchus, swilling wine.
A student sketch, he thinks,
And idly walks behind it, pauses, blinks,
Seeing no canvas, but a printed sign:

Gina, at last I've found
The way to ask you. Will you marry me?
Please say yes. Quickly he looks around,
While angels, saints, the Child on Mary's knee,
Two Popes, aristocrats
In velvet capes and soft tricornered hats
Seem silent partners in the mystery.

Just then a guard comes near
And turns the easel so it can be seen,
As though by covert signal: *Gina's here!*
The tall brunette? The slender girl in green,
So raptly brooding on
The Holy Family with a Young St. John?
The bluejeanned blonde across the mezzanine?

But no, among the rest
An older woman—dark, with deep-set eyes,
Plump, fortyish, unfashionably dressed—
Now gasps, as through the milling crowd she spies
Her name. Cheeks flushed, her hands
Flying to cover them, at first she stands
Transfixed in her confusion and surprise,

Then turns to him—a thin,
Bald, slightly scruffy man, about her age,
One who, like her, could never hope to win
The hearts of strangers glancing from a page
To see him board a train
Or raise his collar higher in the rain,
But who now shares with her a floodlit stage,

A spellbound silence. *Yes,*
She says. Again: *Oh, yes,* and then in tears
Embraces him. At once, as if to bless
A miracle redeeming all their years
Of numbing tedium,
The guards, who'd waited hours for her to come,
Break into smiles and lead the crowd in cheers.

No Angel

All that thou sayest unto me I will do.
—RUTH 3:5

I

The story's strange. For once, God wasn't talking,
Busy with some sacrifice or slaughter
Somewhere else. No plague, cloud, gushing water,
Dream, omen, whirlwind. Just two women, walking
The dusty road from Moab to Judea,
One, the younger, having told the other
(Not her own, but her dead husband's mother)
That she would never leave her. But they flee a
Famine for what, at first, seems something worse:
To come as widows to a teeming city,
To men's appraising stares, and women's pity.
Ruth, the pagan, heard Naomi curse,
Cringed and scanned the sky. No fire or stone
Came crashing downward. They were on their own.

II

Back home (but no, not home) she faced the wall.
"I went out full; empty has God returned me,"
She cried, "And all my piety has earned me
Nothing from Him except the bitter gall
Of shame and grief. He hates me now." Her voice
Quavered and broke. "My name is not Naomi.
You saw them, Ruth. They didn't even know me.
Now leave me be." Ruth did. She had no choice,

Since they were hungry. It was harvest time,
And so she went to glean the fallen wheat
The mowers moving through the fields would miss.
All day ripe kernels rang—plunk, tock, and chime.
Old Boaz watched her stoop in evening heat
To winnow them. "Whose maid," he asked, "is this?"

III

Our hero: stout, gray-bearded, bald. A farmer,
Known for his practicality and thrift.
A bushelful of barley was his gift,
And the order to his servants not to harm her.
Ruth brought the bundle home as he commanded,
Stood at Naomi's bed and spilled the grain
Onto the faded sheets like so much rain,
Laughing, "He wouldn't send me empty-handed!"

Soon afterward, a rustling in the room
One night awakened her. Ruth heard her name.
A lantern spluttered. From behind the flame
An urgent voice enjoined her: "Quick! Get dressed.
No, this one, dear. You want to look your best.
Wear your hair loose. And put on some perfume."

IV

No angel stood there, only her mother-in-law,
Eyeing the bag of roasted grain and scheming,
Foretelling how she'd find him—sprawled and dreaming
Beside the barley sheaves, on bales of straw.
Like wings, she said, his cloak would cover them.
The plan risked everything. But as before—
While aisles of rustling wheatstalks whispered *Whore*—
Ruth walked alone through shuttered Bethlehem.

She stood above him. Started turning. Stayed.
The dozing reapers sighed but did not hear.
Watched by the neutral moon, she watched him stir,
Heard his stuttering snores, and was afraid.
A moment later, God did not appear,
And Boaz wakened to the scent of myrrh.

V

Naomi, meanwhile, follows to the farm's
Long shadows, and with Ruth she hears him laugh.
He lifts the jug again. The windblown chaff
Smokes in the fire, sticking to sweaty arms.
Their bellies full, they drop the blackened ears
And fragrant husks. The torches all burn down.
Now Ruth comes forward, ghostlike in her gown,
And then the bright moon dims and disappears.

What if it failed? The town would turn, reviling
The two of them, its massive gates clang fast.
Then who would take them in? Now she's been gone
Three hours. Now four. Naomi slept at last,
Lost in the cornfields, calling her. At dawn
She woke, and Ruth was in the doorway smiling.

VI

Imagine his surprise, turning to see a
Shivering woman there, her hair a cloud
Of musk that dizzied him. Next day, as proud
As though the whole thing were his own idea,
He married her. Lust? Kindness? Who can tell?
To question too minutely the behavior
Of such a human and unlikely savior
Seems churlish. It's enough all ended well:

In nine months more, Naomi was to dandle
Fat Obed on her lap—the squalling, messy
Grandson who would grow up to father Jesse.
Good rabbis, later on, quailed at the scandal:
King David's great-grandma was not a Jew.
So strange, the story almost must be true.

Rebekah I

I used to listen to him while he prayed,
Wrapped in his father's mantle, for a son,
That God would grant me mercy. There was none.
How bitterly he must have felt betrayed

As ten years passed. Fifteen. Yet never cursed,
Though almost worse than anger was his look
Of baffled sorrow, as the bride he took
From God grew old. Meanwhile I burned with thirst

For him—the sweetness of his sweaty head,
His neck tasting of salt, our secret words,
His sturdy legs, his heartbeat like a bird's.
One night I woke and saw him by my bed—

He'd had a nightmare, and was crying. *There,*
I said, and reached for him. But he was made
Of shadows, and at once began to fade,
And at my touch he turned again to air.

But most nights, now, I lie awake and think,
Twisting the golden bracelet like a charm,
How I let down the pitcher on my arm
And spilled it in the stranger's hands to drink;

And when he'd had his fill, to his surprise
I ran back to the well. There was enough
For all ten camels, kneeling at the trough
With dusty necks, flicking away the flies.

I watch him sleep: no more a wife, a daughter,
Nothing but this one wish between the dry
Immensities of sand and distant sky,
My life contracted to a cry for water.

Rebekah II

And then one night I dreamed I saw a stone
Split open like a melon in the heat,
Its ripe pulp starred with seeds, its juice as sweet
As Jordan's honey. I had been alone

So long that I no longer hoped to feel
Anything stir except my childish heart,
Rocking itself in darkness. At the start
The tremors were too faint to seem quite real,

Faint as a snatch of song, a distant rumor,
Dim intimations of a change in weather,
A flutter like the stroking of a feather.
And then I came to know His sense of humor—

Prayer answered with a vengeance. In my womb
Twin wrestlers struggle, brother jostling brother,
Two nations bent on strangling one another
Before they draw a breath. *There is not room*

For both, I said. *If this be so, what good
Will it do for me?* That was not His concern,
And helplessly I wept and watched Him turn
To go, not caring if I understood.

The elder shall serve the younger one, He said;
So both shall live. And me? I cannot breathe;
While beeswarms hum, corn thickens, crickets seethe,
I hoard my secret knowledge and my dread.

*May you be mother of a myriad
Of sons,* my brother blessed me when I went.
Soon now. I wait beside the open tent
And hear the growl of thunder, fiercely glad.

MARY MAGDALENE

The squabbling soldiers gone, the women got
What fell to them. Beneath the drooping eyes
Of Pilate's guard (the afternoon was hot)
They laid him out and shooed the stinging flies,

Rubbed linen strips with myrrh and aloes, rinsed
The dust from limbs whose wounds no longer bled.
As if the crown still pressed there, Mary winced
When, with a separate cloth, they wrapped his head;

And she recalled the pressure of his palm,
The scent of spikenard, Simon's baleful stare,
And how, the whole house filling with the balm,
She wiped his wet feet with her loosened hair.

Days later, at the empty tomb alone,
She thought first of his pierced and broken feet
And wept, incredulous. But he was gone,
The wrappings, neatly rolled, still faintly sweet.

A gardener was bending in the shade
Among the gravestones. Trembling with dismay,
She cried, "Where is he? Tell me where you've laid
His body. Who has taken him away?"

He didn't answer. When she called again,
The stranger stood and took a step or two.
Her fear became bewilderment. And then
He said her name, and suddenly she knew.

The Feast of Tabernacles

After the final meal hurriedly eaten
Behind doors spattered with lambsblood, sandals and staff
Ready for flight, the rising dough in bowls
Brought on the journey unbaked, the wailing children
Snatched from sleep and huddled into clothes;
After the keening grief when the Egyptians
Found their own children smothered in their beds
Too suddenly for sound, and then the chase
Across the desert to the Sea of Reeds;
After plunging, panicked, through the corridor
Of water impossibly sundered like a chasm
On either side, then seeing the chariots
Of Pharaoh's army roll and disappear,
Shrieking horses and soldiers drowned alike
Under the crumpling walls: after all that,
They must have thought they saw the land of Canaan
Lushly shimmering in the middle distance
Just beyond the column of white smoke—
Never that the high drama of departure
Would be followed by forty years of tedium,
More than fourteen thousand evening meals cooked
And eaten, pots scoured and clothing scrubbed
With never enough water, by stooping women,
While dust and sand got into everything.
Manna, glazing the ground the first morning
Of exile like flakes of hoarfrost, celestial food
Tasting of honey and coriander seed,
Soon grew monotonous as a steady diet.
For Moses, the exclusive interviews
On Sinai punctuated weary years
Of settling quarrels, hearing footsore stragglers
Ask again if they were almost there,
Or grumble resentfully that even bondage

Was better than a life of wandering.
Think how long it must have been before
The death of bitter nostalgia, then of desire
For a promised land that none would ever see;
Longer still before they welcomed joy
To the temporary shelter of the way,
Stars shining through the scattered branches.

V

The Waiting Room

ZERO AT THE BONE

The Diagnosis

For years it hardly moved at all.
It didn't dart, or even creep.
It had no power to appall,
Its hooded eyes eclipsed with sleep.

It didn't dart, or even creep,
Recumbent on a sun-warmed shelf,
Its hooded eyes eclipsed with sleep,
So still, it seemed your very self.

Recumbent on a sun-warmed shelf,
It hadn't will or means to strike,
So still, it seemed your very self
While seconds ticked, each clenched, alike.

It hadn't will or means to strike.
How long it indolently grew,
While seconds ticked, each clenched, alike.
When did it learn to cleave in two?

How long it indolently grew,
How thick! It was a stagnant mass.
When did it learn to cleave in two,
Pouring itself through stones and grass?

How thick it was, a stagnant mass.
What force impelled it to aspire,
Pouring itself through stones and grass,
Purposive, lithe, and swift as fire?

What force impelled it to aspire?
What touched its fuse until it sprang,
Purposive, lithe, and swift as fire?
Then finally the sirens rang.

What touched its fuse? Until it sprang,
It had no power to appall.
Then finally the sirens rang.
For years it hardly moved at all.

The Waiting Room

At first, what most surprises is the silence:
No hum of small talk, no camaraderie,
And never tears or curses. Sorrow's violence
Is dampened to a dull anxiety

That thrums beneath the murmurs of the nurses
And one young couple whispering in Spanish.
Numbly we read, knit, rummage through our purses
For cellphones, crossword puzzles, till we vanish

One at a time behind the frosted door.
Why is it we don't welcome with relief
Familiar faces, names we've heard before,
The knowledge we're not singled out for grief?

Is it reserve? The need to be courageous?
Perhaps we share some superstitious dread
That others' rotten luck might prove contagious?
Or is the fear that hovers here, unsaid,

There's just so much good luck to go around;
She might get mine? Regardless, we don't speak.
Blank-faced commuters rumbling underground,
Our glances cross, impassive and oblique.

Already we've gone farther than we planned.
Will there be such a station as Too Far?
Looking around the room, I understand
What Hope was doing in Pandora's jar.

ULTRASOUND

A dimly lighted room . . . Knees spread and bent
Under the flimsy sheet to make a tent,
And wearing nothing but a paper robe,
I watch him roll a Trojan on a probe
(The condom, here, discreetly called the "cover"),
Reflecting, *Well, a doctor for a lover*
At last, or close enough, and when he wiggles
The wand around, fight off a fit of giggles
(Despite what's called "discomfort") at the thought.
Remote behind his mask, an astronaut,
He turns aside and frowns at the machine.
One sunless planet rises on a screen
Grainy as television's ghostly blue,
And soon its twin moons flicker into view
One at a time. He gestures, and I stare,
Half in surprise. But yes, they're really there,
And they "look fine," he says between my legs—
Two small gray baskets, holding all my eggs.

FRUITLESS

Now oleander flames along the beach
And tart green sea grapes ripen one by one,
While inland, warm and heavy in the sun,
The rosy mangoes dangle out of reach.
Alone these languid afternoons, I teach
Myself the names of trees. We're overrun
With litchi nuts, and then, their season done,
Pick sapodilla, sweet as any peach.

A mass of tangled green, the lawn's gone wild.
Another friend has had another child,
This one (she'd laughed, embarrassed) a surprise.
Small lizards, lithe in torrid silence, dart
Beneath beseeching sprays of bleeding heart
And blue and orange birds-of-paradise.

USEFUL ADVICE

You're 37? Don't you think that maybe
It's time you settled down and had a baby?

No wine? Does this mean happy news? I knew it!

Hey, are you sure you two know how to do it?

All Dennis has to do is look at me
And I'm knocked up.
                        Some things aren't meant to be.
It's sad, but try to see this as God's will.

I've heard that sometimes when you take the Pill—

A friend of mine got pregnant when she stopped
Working so hard.
                        Why don't you two adopt?
You'll have one of your own then, like my niece.

At work I heard about this herb from Greece—

My sister swears by dong quai. Want to try it?

Forget the hightech stuff. Just change your diet.

It's true! Too much caffeine can make you sterile.

Yoga is good for that. My cousin Carol—

They have these ceremonies in Peru—

You mind my asking, is it him or you?

Have you tried acupuncture? Meditation?

It's in your head. Relax! Take a vacation
And have some fun. You think too much. Stop trying.

Did I say something wrong? Why are you crying?

In Glass

A photo for your album

Floating in clear solution in a dish,
How beautiful they are, like cultured pearls,
Pale sequins of some iridescent fish,
Or cloudy globes in which we gaze, foreseeing
Your blue-eyed son, a daughter with my curls,
Frozen halfway from nothingness to being.

Here's the sublime of lab and microscope,
Their sacraments, impalpable to sight.
Half trying, half afraid to summon hope,
We marvel at our colonies of cells—
Four perfect spheres, surrounded by the bright
Coronas of their still-unbroken shells,

Small stars, none more substantial than a wraith,
On which we wish with our agnostic faith.

AFTER ALL

After it all—the tawdry tests; "relations"
(As sexy-sounding as a rubber glove),
When once, before all these humiliations,
We'd blithely fucked or blissfully made love;

The answering service staffed by bored young men;
The days I wept and drank and wouldn't cope;
More pills and more procedures, and again
The dumb resurgence and the death of hope;

The nights when what we were was past recalling;
The days the whole ordeal seemed darkly funny;
After the prayers unanswered, the appalling
Loss of a dream, of dignity, of money—

We have no children. Now beyond despair,
Blue evenings at the kitchen sink, the scent
Of pale night-blooming jasmine in the air,
We know how lavish, how resilient

Love is; and now I see at last (through tears
Of gratitude instead of grief or gall)
That we are fruitful: that, in seven years,
Love's made a family of us, after all.

FLORIDA'S FLOWERS

Even the names of them are sweet—
Moss Rose, Mandevilla, Canna,
Caladium and Poinciana,
Peacock, Pagoda, Passion Flower,
Coral Vine, with tangled stems;
Honey Plant and Glorybower,
Whose berries look like bags of gems;
Hibiscus, crisp in torrid heat;
Pink Allamanda, red Turk's Cap,
Natal Plum, with milky sap
And rosy fruit that you can eat;
Autumn-tinted Copperleaf
That never bears two leaves alike;
Firethorn and Firespike,
Trumpet Creeper, Heavenly Chief,
Pine Cone Ginger, Pride of the Cape,
Brown Sea Oats and green Sea Grape,
Pampas Grass, as sharp as nettles,
Sending up, like ocean spumes,
Its cloudy cotton candy blooms;
Bulbous, funny Dutchman's Pipe;
Crape Myrtle, shirred with crinkled petals;
Ferns of every shape and type—
Staghorn, Hare's Foot, Maidenhair—
Whose powder sifts and gently settles
Snowlike through the humid air;
And everywhere there's Oleander,
That can thrive along the sand or
Crowded roads as well as on
A placid green suburban lawn.

Some of them are bright and showy—
The slender bells of Kalanchoe;
Or the queen of deep July,
Night-blooming Cereus, whose snowy

Flowers loosen as evening falls;
Flame Vine, licking roofs and walls
With orange tongues; or Chalice Vine,
Whose yellow blossoms turn to gold,
Like goblets fit for Cana's wine.

Others are secretive and shy—
Impatiens, happiest in shade;
Candlebush, whose buds unfold
One by one, and slowly fade;
Plumbago, palest of the few
Flowers that Nature painted blue,
The blue of early morning sky.

Some have exotic tales and names—
Mahoe's fragile flowers nod
From gold to red like dying flames;
Ixora, honoring a god,
Is scattered still in Indian shrines;
Naupaka's every bloom was torn,
Says legend, by a lover's scorn
Of one who still laments and pines.

But lovely as the elegant
Or Latinate are common names,
Some whimsical as children's games—
Hen and Chickens, Elephant Ears,
Pelican Flower, Swiss Cheese Plant,
Which peels itself as fruit appears—
A child invented these; and surely
Adam, innocent of art,
Bestowed its name on Bleeding Heart,
On Angel's Trumpet, all its pearly
Poisonous faces gazing down;
Queen's Wreath, King's Mantle, and King's Crown;
And all the flowers sewn with "of"—
Shower-of-Gold and Rain-of-Fire,
Crown-of-Thorns and Chain-of-Love,

Sweet symbols of love's bitter sighs;
And flicking orange wings between
Broad leaves, from guardian sheaths of green,
Blue-headed Bird-of-Paradise.

Bright spirits of a day, an hour,
That insects, storms, and drought devour,
That seem to have but little power,
How irresistible their spell!
Even the names of them enchant—
Moss Rose, Mandevilla, Canna,
Caladium and Poinciana,
Peacock, Pagoda, Passion Flower,
Glorybower and Honey Plant.

First Contact

Small astronaut, no longer than my thumb,
Beached on a *terra nova* red as Mars,
How unimaginably far you've come,
Dreaming of that dark voyage through the stars.

The Dream of Extra Room

The rooms you never knew were there
Wait for you at night.
Some are mere closets, snug and dark,
Some airy, tiled with light.

This one's a ship's prow, pitched and creaking,
That one plain and square,
A third a hive of curious corners
Tucked beneath a stair.

But all are empty and unused,
With an emptiness that rings
Not of what was, but what was not:
No recollection clings

To these blank walls that could have held
Guests' babble, steaming food,
A bedroom for a second child,
A brooding solitude.

But you, though richer than you knew,
Were still too small to see
The cunningly constructed door
That lay, uncannily,

So near as you deplored your lot.
No wonder, then, you stand
Stricken with wonder as, unlocked,
It yields beneath your hand.

TWENTY WEEKS

For my daughter, February 22, 2001

Sophie Rose, still folded tight
This windy February night,
Your fists like buds, your deep eyes shut,
This day another rose was cut
Nearly sixty years ago,
A century you'll never know
But think of (so I hope) at school
As ancient, atavistic, cruel.

The night before she died, she dreamed
She walked a mountain path. Light gleamed
Among the leaves that seemed to leap
And dart like fish. The trail was steep,
Foreboding, though the sun was mild.
But she held firmly to the child
She carried, in a christening gown,
Toward a church in a village town
Perched on the sloping mountainside.
Then suddenly there opened wide
A deep crevasse beneath her feet.
Unable either to retreat
Down the way she'd come, or climb
Out of danger, she'd only time,
As it became a broad abyss,
To lean across the precipice
And save the child before she fell.
Next morning, in her prison cell,
Excited, flushed and confident,
She told her cellmate what it meant:

The dream described here was related by Sophie Scholl, of the White Rose resistance group, to her cellmate on the morning of February 22, 1943, the day a Nazi court convicted and executed her for treason.

"The child is our idea: we
Have carried it, privileged to be
Forerunners, and to testify
For freedom. Though we now must die,
The child we nurtured will live on,
Cherished by others when we're gone."

Your great-grandmother, another Rose,
Was born among White Russian snows,
But crossed the sea at seventeen,
Transplanted to the unforeseen
Though dreamed of. With what wondering fear
She must have seen them looming near—
The towers at Manhattan's edge;
The harpstrings of the Brooklyn Bridge,
Wind-swept; colossal Liberty;
The broad piers of the Battery.
There, released in a jostling mob,
She went to school and found a job,
Married for love during the War,
Raised her children and kept the store,
Living on makeshift furniture
Behind it when they were too poor
For rent, and in the times of camps
And pogroms, lit memorial lamps,
Baked bread and kept the holidays,
Banked fires, made Sabbath candles blaze.
Her house, each Friday, was an ark
Of light that rode the rising dark,
Her life a history of these
Small ordinary decencies
Fanatics scorn and war obscures,
Without which nothing good endures.

May you be grafted from these two,
A hybrid bloom, Catholic and Jew
Commingled in one hardy shoot
From which you'll grow, the first, sweet fruit.
Midsummer flower, may you be

Transfiguringly kind as she
Who gave her life, and she who gave
Life to others. May you have,
Like them, and like your counterpart
The rose, tough roots and tender heart,
A strength like theirs your anchorage;
And may you live to a great age
As someone named for wisdom should,
Lost years the other Sophie would
Have had, your gift. In every weather,
Wisdom and grace guard you together
And shelter you from harm and storm,
Who now lie heedless, dreamless, warm,
Curled in your dark honeycomb
Asleep, exactly halfway home.

THIS CHILD

This child, in whose improbable red hair
My mother soon will see a fair colleen—
The dormant Shea genes slipped from quarantine—
While yours will find a beauty to compare
With her own mother Rose, a *gingy* too,
Belongs, for this first night, to me and you.

Strait-jacketed, the sometime acrobat
Lies still now, punch-drunk from the din and glare
That hauled her howling, flailing, from her lair
Like a furious pink rabbit from a hat.
She has fine lungs (Italian, we suppose),
Whether an Irish or a Jewish Rose.

So furtively you'd think a watchful warden
Might interrupt, we pull the cap away—
Conspirators again, as on the day
We took our vows in the judge's tiny garden,
Hopeful and ignorant of what they'd mean,
Framed with magnolia's cream and tangled green.

She's really here, resistant as the world,
Marvelous as an unexpected joke,
A gift to be unwrapped. Shyly we stroke
Damp head, clown feet, tease starfish hands uncurled,
That copper down, startlingly bright and fine,
Closing the circuit between your hand and mine.

Meanwhile, neither of her world nor of this,
She gazes past us, toward the sunless void
She'd crossed to meet us like an asteroid—
The proof of an absurd hypothesis
We'd stubbornly defended all the same,
While all the time we hoarded this pure flame.

USEFUL ADVICE, THE SEQUEL

Eastern Parkway Station

The token vendor hunkered in her booth
Surveys the homebound throng through plexiglass
Like a fortuneteller brooding on the truth,
Then booms some admonition as I pass,
Or rather, we—she's curled against my chest,
Lulled by the train's long shudder into rest.

Startled, I turn (*Who, me?*) and meet her eye;
She beckons, nods. By now I could have been
Halfway up to the mild September sky,
But I shuffle toward her till, above the din,
The intercom assaults again: *I said,
I hope you going to cover that baby's head!*

Liana's Song

based on the song of the fairies from
A Midsummer Night's Dream

Who rides so late through wind and dark,
    Dreaming girl, with streaming hair?
Swollen stormclouds, hold, and hark,
    Spirits of the earth and air:

Crickets, sing her where she's bound,
Silkworms, keep her warmly gowned.
Gather, gather, gather 'round, from above and underground,
    Fireflies light
    Her way tonight,
Circle her without a sound,
Wind her horse and moon her hound.

Spiders with a hundred eyes,
    Trees with boughs like creaking spars,
Watch her, rock her, while she lies,
    Sailor in a ship of stars.

Crickets, sing her where she's bound,
Silkworms, keep her warmly gowned.
Gather, gather, gather 'round, from above and underground,
    Fireflies light
    Her way tonight,
Circle her without a sound,
Wind her horse and moon her hound,

Till the shadows on the lawn
Shine with dew at ruddy dawn.

First Sight

I dreamed your face before we met,
A face familiar as my own.
Love was an effortless duet

For us, when, from a silhouette—
A fog around phosphoric bone—
I dreamed your face, before we met;

But when you surfaced, bruised and wet,
Your gaze was no one's I had known.
And so began a strained duet

Marred by false starts, wrong notes, regret,
Through which (love gone, or not yet grown)
I dreamed your face. Before we met,

You were a ghost. You hold me yet,
Substantial now as any stone.
How long we practiced our duet,

How slowly learned love's alphabet.
How long ago, asleep, alone,
I dreamed your face—before we met,
And started this undreamt duet.

Selected by Robert Fink, *Keeping My Name* is the thirteenth winner of the Walt McDonald First-Book Competition in Poetry. The competition is supported generously through donated subscriptions from *The American Scholar, The Atlantic Monthly, The Georgia Review, Gulf Coast, The Hudson Review, The Massachusetts Review, Poetry, Shenandoah,* and *The Southern Review.*